RULES OF S.U.R.V.I.V.A.L.

BY REGINALD E. ROBINSON

RULES OF SURVIVAL by Reginald E. Robinson
published by Watersprings Publishing,
a division of Watersprings Media House, LLC.
P.O. Box 1284 Olive Branch, MS 38654
www.waterspringspublishing.com
Contact publisher for bulk orders and permission requests.

Copyright © 2023 Reginald E. Robinson. All rights reserved. No part of this publication may be reproduced, distributed, or transmitted in any form or by any means, including photocopying, recording, or other electronic or mechanical methods, without the prior written permission of the publisher, except in the case of brief quotations embodied in critical reviews and certain other noncommercial uses permitted by copyright law.

Scripture quotations marked (NLT) are taken from the Holy Bible, New Living Translation, copyright © 1996. Used by permission of Tyndale House Publishers, Inc., Wheaton, IL 60189 USA. All rights reserved.

Scripture quotations credited to NIV are from the Holy Bible, New International Version. Copyright © 1973, 1978, 1984, 2011 by Biblica, Inc. Used by permission. All rights reserved worldwide.

Scripture quotations credited to NASB are from the New American Standard Bible, copyright © 1960, 1962, 1963, 1968, 1971, 1972, 1973, 1975, by the Lockman Foundation. Used by permission.

Scripture quotations marked "NKJV" are taken from the New King James Version. Copyright © 1982 by Thomas Nelson, Inc. Used by permission. All rights reserved

Printed in the United States of America.

ISBN-13: 978-1-948877-96-1

Words of Praise for Rules of SURVIVAL

You are holding in your hands an essential resource for anyone seeking to know the keys to a meaningful life. If you apply the principles compiled in this book, I am totally convinced that your life will be filled with meaning and purpose.

Dr. Christopher C. Thompson
Author and Adjunct Professor at Oakwood University

In *Rules of S.U.R.V.I.V.A.L* Pastor Robinson does a phenomenal job of making the big picture of faith practical for everyday living. Each chapter reads like an effective tool or weapon to pick up for the very real struggle of day-to-day life. Reginald keeps things simple and straightforward for this journey and uses a number of effective illustrations and metaphors to highlight and drive each point home.

Jason Francis **Founder of Kinetic**

Rules of S.U.R.V.I.V.A.L.

By Reginald E. Robinson

DEDICATION

This book is dedicated to my wife, Cynthia. She encouraged me to write this book, and her love and support have empowered me to pursue many things in ministry I never thought were possible. Cynthia pushes me to constantly improve, grow in God, and allow Him to lead wherever He takes me—and us.

ACKNOWLEDGEMENTS

Edna Robinson, my mom, has always been in my corner, showing support and love. She always advised me to follow God, even when some of the decisions I made while following God and doing His will did not make sense to her.

Bonnie Beres, thanks for editing, reading, and rereading my manuscript. Even when things were not clear, you still made it happen. Thank you for being willing to help me out despite all the other things you do in your busy life.

CONTENTS

Preface xiii

1. S: Size Up the Situation 1

2. U: Undue Haste Makes Waste 7

3. R: Relinquish; Let Go of Fear and Panic 13

4. V: Victorious Living in Christ 21

5. I: Invite the Holy Spirit In 27

6. V: Value Christian Living 31

7. A: Act Like a Native 35

8. L: Live for Jesus 39

About the Author 45

PREFACE

While I was praying one day, wondering how I could impact the world, those in my circle, and those I will come in contact with, it hit me: write a book. And I thought, *Write a book? Me?* And I laughed. *What could I possibly have to say?*

I continued praying, and another thought hit me — this time, like a ton of bricks. *You have to turn the 'Rules of Survival' into a book.*

The concept behind "Rules of S.U.R.V.I.V.A.L" first came to me while reflecting on my past. While attending Oakwood College (now Oakwood University) in Huntsville, AL., I worked at the U.S. Space & Rocket Center. A class called "Rules of Survival" was a part of my training for work at the center.

Not too many years later, after accepting an invitation to preach, the Holy Spirit recalled those words to me: "Rules of S.U.R.V.I.V.A.L." It was the first time I would preach a sermon on survival.

Since then, I have preached the Rules of S.U.R.V.I.V.A.L several times. The Lord even led me to develop a video presentation. For the sermon and the presentation, as well as in the book you're now reading, the word "SURVIVAL" is used as an acronym.

I have been doing nothing but praying since I began typing the first word on the first page of what has become this book. My prayer is that "Rules of S.U.R.V.I.V.A.L" will reassure you, the reader, in your daily walk with Christ—to help you to know you *can* survive in this world. Even when it seems Satan has taken over, God is still in control.

CHAPTER 1

S:
SIZE UP THE SITUATION

People are expected to make decisions in life. But without knowing all the information, or when operating on half-cocked information, people cannot make *informed* decisions—the types of decisions most beneficial to them. A decision that is made without all of the information is likely to be improper and misinformed.

When you understand what is happening around you, you are equipped to make better decisions. For example, if you knew before you acted that just one drink, or just one puff, or just one one-night stand would lead to lifelong struggle, you might choose to prevent the future hardship.

When I was a teenager, I made a misinformed decision based on what was going on around me. For example, I was never all that good at basketball, but my friends and I played tip-out basketball one afternoon.

One of the rules of tip-out basketball is that when another person misses a shot, you can catch the ball and shoot—without dribbling. If you make your shot, the other person is out.

We were playing in a gymnasium that had a stage at the side of the court. I was on the stage when the shot was missed. I had two options: try to make the basket from the stage; or jump off the stage and shoot the ball while in the air. Guess what I chose?

I jumped and shot the ball in midair.

It didn't turn out well. I hit the floor, twisted my knee, and was in a leg brace for two months—not to mention the hospital bill my mother had to pay.

If I had taken an extra moment that day to size up the situation, there would not have been a leg brace, nor a hospital bill, nor me hitting the floor.

Think about it. If you size up the situation, it can save you a lot of heartache and pain. In addition, you can prevent a lot of bad habits and difficult issues in your life if you take just an extra moment to size up the situation.

Regardless of the situation, it's essential to get clear on the decision that needs to be made, what factors are helping you decide, and the effects of that decision. So here are some questions to help you size up the situation:

S: Size Up the Situation

1. What is the entire situation?
2. What are the effects of this situation in your life?
3. What effect is the decision you make going to have on your walk with Christ?
4. What is helping you make this decision (e.g., friends, parents, Bible, social media)?

What are the benefits of sizing up the situation? Examining your thought process in this way can:

1. Make you aware of your surroundings and the influences that help you make decisions in life.
2. Tell you where you stand in your relationship with God and the world.
3. Illustrate the condition that you are living in and the decisions you are making and/or need to be making.
4. Allow you the space to see there are two sides to every situation.
5. Give you hope when things around you are hopeless and sad.
6. Inspire you to make good decisions, regardless of what is around you.
7. Let you know you are not alone.
8. Reassure you that when Christ is for you, it's OK if the world is against you.
9. Preserve your hope in Jesus.

As Christians, when we size up the situation and look around, it becomes apparent that the earth we live in is filled with sin.

One of the stories in the Bible that best describes sizing up the situation is in Daniel chapters 1-3. It tells the story of four young men who counted the cost of following God and made the right choices. The story reaches its apex when these young men are confronted with a decision: will they bow to the king or remain standing?

They chose to stand on the side of Christ and remained standing, even when everyone else—their mothers and fathers, their uncles and aunties, and many other people they respected—bowed. Even after being given several chances to change their mind, the young men counted the cost and made a pivotal move. They did not bow.

Even when faced with death, their response—after sizing up the situation—is recorded in Daniel 3:17-18 when they say, *"If it be so, our God whom we serve is able to deliver us from the burning fiery furnace, and he will deliver us out of thine hand, O king. But if not, be it known unto thee, O king, that we will not serve thy gods, nor worship the golden image which thou hast set up."* (KJV)

Here are some additional Bible verses to examine when you have to size up the situation:

S: Size Up the Situation

Romans 3:22 – *"For all have sinned and come short of the glory of God."* (KJV)

Psalms 51:5 – *"True, I was born a sinner from the moment my mother conceived me."* (TLB)

Romans 6:23 – *"For the wages of sin is death; but the gift of God is eternal life through Jesus Christ our Lord."* (KJV)

Romans 8:31 – *"What shall we then say to these things? If God be for us, who can be against us?"* (KJV)

John 3: 16-17 – *"For God so loved the world, that he gave his only begotten Son, that whosoever believeth in him should not perish, but have everlasting life. For God sent not his Son into the world to condemn the world; but that the world through him might be saved."* (KJV)

Now you can see how important it is that we understand what is surrounding a situation. Our knowledge will help us to make a good, or a Great, choice.

Count the cost, now and in the future. Your choices today *will* affect tomorrow-size up the situation.

NOTE PAGE

CHAPTER 2

U:
Undue Haste Makes Waste

Once there was a hunter who lived in a village with his very faithful dog. One day, the hunter went to the city with his wife. They left their son at home. While they were gone, a wolf found its way into the house and attacked the boy. The faithful dog fought the wolf and killed it.

When the hunter and his wife returned from the city in the evening, the dog was waiting outside. When the dog saw his master, he began to lick his feet. The hunter then saw the stains of blood on the dog's mouth.

The hunter thought the dog had killed his son, and he became irate; he took his gun and killed the dog. The hunter then went inside, where he found his son safe in the house with a wolf lying dead near him. He wept bitterly.[1]

---

[1] This folk tale, widely known in the United States as "A Hunter and His Faithful Dog," is frequently used to teach the proverb "haste makes waste." Origin unknown. Text is available at Answers.com and elsewhere.

In this story, the hunter did not take the time to find out what was really going on — and it cost the life of his dog. The hunter's haste wasted the life of his faithful dog, the protector of his child. We all have made decisions under pressure or in a hurry, and after we thought about it, we knew it was not the right choice to make.

Maybe you've been hanging out with your friends, and then someone pulls out a pornographic magazine. All it takes is one look, and sin gets its hooks in you. Instead of leaving, you decide to stay. This decision isn't something you think about; it is made in haste.

Or, maybe every other girl is going to Third Base with the football team, and they shame you into doing something you know is not right. You make a hasty decision.

There are always people who are going to try to rush you into making a decision. And when you act with haste, you can lose and waste so much.

To prevent this, allow me to suggest something: slow down!

You don't need to rush through life like you are going to miss out on something. Do not allow music, the media, or others around you to rush you into choosing sex, drugs, or alcohol. Most people use these things as a way to cope with their own hasty and wasteful decisions.

U: Undue Haste Makes Waste

The following nine things show how rushing, or undue haste, can create waste:

1. Rushing causes you to make mistakes and even forget things.
2. Rushing can cause you to run past God's plan.
3. We rush the Sabbath to come during the week, and when it gets here, we rush it away.
4. Devotions during the week can be rushed.
5. We will not know God's plan if we rush.
6. We cannot hear God's voice when we're in a rush.
7. When we rush, how will we know it is He that is speaking, and not we convincing ourselves that it is He?
8. We can save ourselves a lot of problems if we slow down and listen.
9. We can get clear instructions if we take time to slow down and listen.

There are examples in the Bible where people were told to wait, stand still and be anxious for nothing.

Exodus 14:13 – *"And Moses said unto the people, Fear ye not, stand still, and see the salvation of the LORD, which he will show to you today: for the Egyptians whom ye have seen today, ye shall see them again no more forever."* (KJV)

Maybe now you are thinking, as the children of Israel said to Moses: "But you don't understand."

I do.

And God does.

Stand still.

Standing still means being talked about; it means not being in the cool circle; it means being laughed at. God will deliver you—just like He did the children of Israel.

> **Philippians 4:6** – *"Be anxious for nothing, but in everything by prayer and supplication with thanksgiving let your requests be made known to God."* (NKJV)
>
> **Psalm 27:14** – *"Wait on the LORD: be of good courage, and he shall strengthen thine heart: wait, I say, on the LORD."* (KJV)
>
> **Isaiah 40:31** – *"But they that wait upon the LORD shall renew their strength; they shall mount up with wings as eagles; they shall run, and not be weary; and they shall walk, and not faint."* (KJV)

When you rush, you run the risk of making a misguided or misinformed decision that can follow you for the rest of your life. The decisions you are making today affect who you are going to be tomorrow.

Your future depends on the decisions that you are making today, so do not allow your friends to rush you into sex, drinking, drugs, or a lifestyle you know is wrong. Know all you need to know to make an informed decision. And slow down! You do not have to experience everything.

NOTE PAGE

CHAPTER 3

R:

RELINQUISH/LET GO OF FEAR AND PANIC

Two explorers were on a jungle safari when suddenly a ferocious lion jumped in front of them.

"Keep calm," the first explorer whispered. "Remember what we read in that book on wild animals? If you stand perfectly still and look the lion in the eye, it will turn and run."

"Sure," replied his companion, "you've read the book, and I've read the book—but has the *lion* read the book?"[2]

While this story is funny, fear is not a laughing matter.

---

[2] "Sermon Illustrations." Sermon Illustrations. http//www.sermonillustrations.com/a-z/fear.htm (accessed April 23, 2014). Currently available at http://www.sermonillustrations.com/a-z/f/fear.htm (2021).

According to Dictionary.com, fear is a noun and a verb. When used as a noun, fear is "a distressing emotion, aroused by impending danger, evil or pain."

This leads me to think of the verse in 1 Peter 5:8, *"Be sober, be vigilant; because your adversary the devil walks about like a roaring lion, seeking whom he may devour."* (NKJV)

Fear is paralyzing — and by the time you figure out what is happening, it is often too late, and you are in a situation you never thought you would be in.

One way to avoid this kind of harm is to not give in to the pressure. Don't give someone else power to the point where they instill fear in you, and you decide to get involved in something that goes against your morals.

When used as a verb, fear is defined as "to regard with fear, be afraid of, a feeling of dread." When you look at it in this sense, God has promised us in **Deuteronomy 31:6**, "Be strong and of good courage, do not fear nor be afraid for them; for the LORD your God, He is the one who goes with you. He will not leave you nor forsake you." (NKJV)

Other verses on the topic of fear include:

> **Deuteronomy 8:5-7** – *"Thou shalt also consider in thine heart, that, as a man chasteneth his son, so the Lord thy God chasteneth thee. Therefore thou shalt keep the commandments of the Lord thy God, to walk in his ways, and to fear him. For the Lord*

thy God bringeth thee into a good land, a land of brooks of water, of fountains and depths that spring out of valleys and hills." (KJV)

Joshua 1:5 – *"There shall not any man be able to stand before thee all the days of thy life: as I was with Moses, so I will be with thee: I will not fail thee, nor forsake thee."* (KJV)

1 Chronicles 28:20 – *"And David said to Solomon his son, Be strong and of good courage, and do it: fear not, nor be dismayed: for the LORD God, even my God, will be with thee; he will not fail thee, nor forsake thee, until thou hast finished all the work for the service of the house of the LORD."* (KJV)

Psalm 37:28 – *"For the LORD loveth judgment, and forsaketh not his saints; they are preserved for ever: but the seed of the wicked shall be cut off."* (KJV)

Psalm 94:14 – *"For the LORD will not cast off his people, neither will he forsake his inheritance."* (KJV)

Isaiah 41:17 – *"When the poor and needy seek water, and there is none, and their tongue faileth for thirst, I the LORD will hear them, I the God of Israel will not forsake them."* (KJV)

Isaiah 42:16 – *"And I will bring the blind by a way that they knew not; I will lead them in paths that they have not known: I will make darkness light before them, and crooked things straight. These things will I do unto them, and not forsake them."* (KJV)

Hebrews 13:5 – *"Let your conversation be without covetousness; and be content with such things as ye have: for he hath said, I will never leave thee, nor forsake thee."* (KJV)

Now that we know what fear is, as a noun and a verb, what does fear make us do? Fear can make us:

1. Not move forward with God.
2. Embrace the very thing that we say we love because of fear.
3. Unwilling to stand up when the time comes.
4. Conform to the rest of the world.
5. Go along with what everyone else is doing.
6. Unable to think straight.

Satan wants your mind not to be clear. Where does help to relinquish fear and panic come from? The three Hebrew boys in the book of Daniel were not afraid to stand, even when faced with death. (Their response was, "Whether God delivers us or not, we still will not bow.") Daniel was not afraid to open his window and pray, even though it got him put in a lions' den.

1 Samuel 17 tells the story of David not fearing like the rest of the army of Israel (even the king) and that helped him save a nation. David trusted more in God than in fear.

In **Revelation 2:8-11**, God tells the church of Smyrna not to fear what they were about to suffer.

What else does the Bible say about fear?

2 Timothy 1:7 – *"For God has not given us the Spirit of fear, but of power and of love and of a sound mind."* (NKJV)

Matthew 10:28 – *"Do not fear those who kill the body but cannot kill the soul. But rather fear Him who is able to destroy both soul and body in hell."* (NKJV)

Psalm 46:1-2 – *"God is our refuge and strength, a very present help in trouble. Therefore will not we fear, though the earth be removed, and though the mountains be carried into the midst of the sea."* (KJV)

2 Samuel 22:3 – *"The God of my rock; in him will I trust: he is my shield, and the horn of my* *salvation, my high tower, and my refuge, my savior; thou savest me from violence."* (KJV)

Psalm 91:4-7 – *"He will cover you with his feathers, and under his wings you will find refuge; his faithfulness will be your shield and rampart. You will not fear the terror of night, nor the arrow that flies by day, nor the pestilence that stalks in the darkness, nor the plague that destroys at midday. A thousand may fall at your side, ten thousand at your right hand, but it will not come near you."*
(NIV)

So, you see from these Bible verses that you are connected to Christ. You have nothing to be afraid of, and you can be bold and walk without fear, just like David stated in **Psalm 23**: "Yea, though I walk through the valley of the shadow of death, I will fear no evil; For You [God] are with me; Your rod and Your staff, they comfort me." (NKJV)

In closing, Kirk Franklin describes confronting fear in his song, "Hello Fear." The lyrics of this song deal with the eviction of fear from your life, saying hello to grace and allowing grace to come and take fear's place.

R: Relinquish/Let Go of Fear and Panic

NOTE PAGE

NOTE PAGE

CHAPTER 4

V:
VICTORIOUS LIVING IN CHRIST

When a sports team wins, I never really hear the athletes talk about what they as an individual did; instead, they always refer to what the team did and the critical role they played as a part of the team. Things like "We won the game," and "We have a great offense," or "We had a great defense" are common.

Satan wants you the think you can do everything by yourself—that you can make it in this world by yourself. You may feel like you can overcome sin, you can overcome life's problems, you can overcome heartaches and pain and confusion and disappointment all by yourself; you do not need help.

Or, you might say to yourself, "I got this; I have been in church all my life. My mom took me to church, and my grandmother took me to church; I've served in the church; I learned all the Bible verses in Vacation Bible School."

But at the end of it all, we all need someone while we are on this earth.

> "People need people. Laurie was about three when one night she requested my aid in getting undressed. I was downstairs, and she was upstairs, and...well.
>
> "You know how to undress," I reminded.
>
> "Yes," she explained, 'but sometimes people need people anyway, even if they do know how to do things by themselves."[3] — William C. Schultz

When it comes to living for Christ, we need His help.

Why? Here is what the Bible says:

> **Psalm 51:5** – *"Behold, I was shapen in iniquity [sin]; and in sin did my mother conceive me."* (KJV)

> **Romans 3:23** – *"for all have sinned and fallen short of the glory of God"* (NASB)

From these verses, we may appear doomed from the word go, but that is not the truth. We can have

---

[3] William C. Schultz, *Bits & Pieces*, December 1990. Copyright ©1996-2020 Bible.org; reprinted with permission.

V: Victorious Living in Christ

victory over sin and what we have been born into. In order to have this victory in life, you have to be a part of Christ, and Christ has to be in you.

The victory comes to those that are in Christ. *He is in you.*

Outside of Christ, there is no victory; you can only count on yourself to do good for so long. Therefore, you have to believe in something greater than yourself, something that has more power than you, to have victory.

This reminds me of a Gatorade commercial. In the commercial, you see an athlete working hard and sweating. The athlete's sweat is the color of the Gatorade they are drinking.

The commercial ends with the question, "Is it in you?" The message is that Gatorade is so much a part of the athlete that it comes out of them.

In order for us to have victorious living in Christ, it will have to be in us. It is going to have to be a part of you. It needs to be what people see when the pressure is on when you are around your friends, and you have to stand.

Is it in you?

Because, to be honest, what is in you will come out of you—and if Christ is not in you, the result will not be a Christian response but a response that will lead to guilt, shame, and a feeling of disconnection from God.

> **2 Corinthians 5:15-21** – *"And He died for all, that those who live should no longer live for themselves but for him who died for them and was raised again. So from now on we regard no one from a worldly point of view. Though we once regarded Christ in this way, we do so no longer. Therefore, if anyone is in Christ, the new creation has come: The old has gone, the new is here! All this is from God, who reconciled us to himself through Christ and gave us the ministry of reconciliation: that God was reconciling the world to himself in Christ, not counting people's sins against them. And he has committed to us the message of reconciliation. We are therefore Christ's ambassadors, as though God were making his appeal through us. We implore you on Christ's behalf: Be reconciled to God. God made him who had no sin to be sin for us, so that in him we might become the righteousness of God."*
> (NIV)

How do you have victorious living in Christ?

You have to live for Him and ask the Holy Spirit to go with you on your day-to-day journey. That means, if you have to get up early to pray, then you do that; if you have to read your Bible a little more, you do that; if you have to ask God to reveal Himself to you, then you do that. Whatever it takes that gives you victory, find it—and do it.

Every time the children of Israel went into battle without God, they lost the battle. Victory is only through Jesus, not through our power and might.

Victorious living continues in your everyday life. Because you do things differently, your friends and family will notice—and that gives you the chance to tell of God's goodness and glory and how He changed your life.

NOTE PAGE

CHAPTER 5

I:
INVITE THE HOLY SPIRIT IN

He just finished arguing with his fiancé, and now it's 3:00 in the morning. When he should be asleep, he is up—still angry, flipping through the TV channels. He flips and flips, and he stops at a channel that speaks to his vulnerability. He knows that he has no business watching, but he stays there and fills his imagination with the very thing that will not help his relationship with Christ—or with his future spouse. Every time there is an argument, he visits that place in his mind, where there is no talking back, no disagreement, whatever he wants done is done. This is the very place that destroys, shatters, and breaks his soul.

She is in that spot again, after dinner or prom, after the movie, party, or game. The back seat of the car, the hotel room—it no longer serves its intended purpose but has now become a bed to fulfill an uncontrollable passion that God intended for married couples.

Both of these individuals have come to a point in their lives where they feel spiritually broken and fed up—and they realize it. What should they do?

They need to ask the Lord for the Holy Spirit to help. They have to invite the Holy Spirit in to have victory in their everyday lives and in the moments when it is the darkest. The Holy Spirit will be the buffer that can help them before trouble even starts.

When you invite the Holy Spirit in, He becomes your moral GPS. When we do not listen, we run the risk, like the seven churches, of removing the Holy Spirit. It becomes a part of you and your actions and your thinking.

1 Corinthians 6:19 – *"Or do you not know that your body is a temple of the Holy Spirit within you, whom you have from God, and that you are not your own?"* (NASB)

Life can get noisy and crowded, and we can get distracted, but God is right there knocking and waiting for us to open the door.

Revelation 3:20 – *"Behold, I stand at the door and knock; if anyone hears My voice and opens the door, I will come in to him and dine with him, and he with Me."* (NASB)

I: Invite the Holy Spirit In

The interesting thing is that God is knocking, and the Holy Spirit is there to help, but neither one of Them is going to intrude and or make you invite Them in... you have to open the door to God and invite the Holy Spirit in.

You may ask yourself, "How will it help me? What is the benefit?"

> **John 14:26-27** – *"But the Counselor, the Holy Spirit, whom the Father will send in my name, will teach you all things and will remind you of everything I have told you."* (CSB)

The Holy Spirit is there to help you, lead, guide, and provide you strength in everyday life.

> **Luke 12:11-12** – *"When you are brought before synagogues, rulers and authorities, do not worry about how you will defend yourselves or what you will say, for the Holy Spirit will teach you at that time what you should say."* (NIV)

This works even when your friends ask why you do the things you do. When you invite the Holy Spirit in, you will change.

How do you invite in the Holy Spirit?

1. PRAY. Give the Holy Spirit permission to lead.
2. ASK the Holy Spirit to speak above the noise of everyday life.
3. LISTEN. Listen for the Holy Spirit to speak.

NOTE PAGE

CHAPTER 6

V:
VALUE CHRISTIAN LIVING

It was a crystal vase, but it was not just any crystal vase. It was handmade and cut to design for Mr. and Mrs. Smith. It was precious; indeed, it was one-of-a-kind. You could see the smallest detail, and many were captivated by its splendor.

It held a special value because it symbolized 50 years of wedded bliss—50 years of watching sunsets, 50 years of love and romance with her high school sweetheart, 50 years with her gift from God.

Mr. Smith passed away about two years earlier, and the vase was a constant reminder of what she had with her husband. It sat on her fireplace mantle so that when Mrs. Smith was having a bad day, good memories could brighten her spirits.

But while she was on vacation visiting the grandkids, someone broke into the house and stole many things. In the process, they knocked over the vase. It shattered into hundreds of pieces.

Mrs. Smith collected all the pieces she could find and went back to the person that made the vase for her, asking him if it could be fixed. He said yes, but explained it would never be whole again; there would always be evidence of the broken pieces. The cost of the repair did not matter. The vase was beyond price—it was the only earthly thing she valued.

When a person values a possession, like clothes, car, phone, tablet, or anything else, they do whatever it takes to care for it and keep it in tip-top shape. If anything goes wrong, it is fixed immediately because they value it.

Remember this:

You are not ashamed of things you value.
You take care of the things you value.
Things you value have a special place.
You are no longer living for yourself but the thing you value.
You seek after the thing you value.
You would be willing to die for the thing you value.

Jesus had enough love and valued us enough that He came and died for us on the cross so that we would not have to face the consequences of our sins.

> **Romans 6:23** – *"For the wages of sin is death, but the free gift of God is eternal life in Christ Jesus our LORD."* (NLT) Jesus loved and valued us so much that He was willing to die for us.

V: Value Christian Living

You will die to protect the things you value. Cars we value break down, and we fix them, regardless of the cost. Gifts from our mom or dad, our favorite uncle — we hold on to these things for years, even when they are broken — because, to us, they have value.

How do you show you value Christian living?

> **1 Peter 2:9** – *"But ye are a chosen generation, a royal priesthood, a holy nation, a peculiar people; that ye should show forth the praises of him who hath called you out of darkness into his marvelous light."* (KJV)

This verse gives a description of a person that values Christian living.

What do you have to do in order to value Christian living?

> **Galatians 2:20** – *"I am crucified with Christ: nevertheless I live; yet not I, but Christ liveth in me: and the life which I now live in the flesh I live by the faith of the Son of God, who loved me, and gave himself for me."* (KJV)

> **Philippians 1:21** – *"For me to live is Christ, and to die is gain."* (KJV)

How can I have victory in death? It comes from dying to self and allowing the Lord to lead you. Your victory is in you dying to self and living for Christ.

NOTE PAGE

CHAPTER 7

A:
ACT LIKE A NATIVE

Natives never give in, regardless of what is around them. Israel conformed to what was happening around them: "Give us a king!" They begged. They were told, "He will use you and make you slaves, he will take your possessions and make slaves out of your children." They replied, "It does not matter… give us a king!" When you do not act like a native of God's Kingdom, you will be willing to accept anything.

If there was any group of people in the Bible that acted like natives, it was Daniel and the three Hebrew boys in **Daniel 1:11-19** and **Daniel 3:16-30**. Even David in **1 Samuel 17**.

These stories are about people who did not conform to their surroundings even though they were the only ones to stand. They realized it was essential to stand for God and not bow before man. They were setting the standard for the world instead of the world setting the standard for them.

> **Romans 12:2** – *"And not be conformed to this world, but be transformed by the renewing of your mind, so that you may prove what they will of God is, that which is a good and acceptable and perfect."* (NASB)

> **1 John 2:15** – *"Don't love the world nor the things in the world. If anyone loves the world, the love of the Father is not in him."* (NASB)

Natives are never ashamed of where they are from. Natives always represent their homeland and do not care what your opinion is of their homeland. Regardless of how pretty or how unattractive—even when it is not the popular thing to do—they still love and live and will die for their homeland.

> **2 Corinthians 5:20** – *"Now then, we are ambassadors for Christ, as though God were pleading through us; we implore you on Christ's behalf, be reconciled to God."* (NKJV)

Max Lucado, in his book "Come Thirsty," sums up one of the problems that arises when you are not living like heaven is your home. Lucado writes, "What a deformed man/woman sin has made you. God created us a little better than angels and Sin has made us a little better than Devils."[4]

> **Philippians 3:17-21** – *"Dear brothers and sisters, pattern your lives after mine, and learn from those who follow our example. For I have told you often before, and I say it again with tears in my eyes, that there are many whose conduct shows they are enemies of the cross of Christ. They are headed for destruction. Their god is their appetite, they brag about shameful things, and they think only about this life here on earth. But we are citizens of heaven, where the Lord Jesus Christ lives. And we are eagerly waiting for him to return as our Savior. He will take our weak mortal bodies and change them into glorious bodies like his own, using the same power with which he will bring everything under his control."* (NLT)

The way you show that you are not an enemy of Christ is by your actions.

---

[4] Excerpt from "Come Thirsty: No Heart Too Dry for His Touch" by Max Lucado. Thomas Nelson, publisher. Reprint Ed. Released April 30, 2012.

NOTE PAGE

CHAPTER 8

L:
LIVE FOR JESUS

There are many things that you can live for that have no lasting value, will not prolong life, and do not have the power to give you eternal life.

And there is one thing that can- living for Jesus. You live for Christ on this earth, and then you get the gift of eternal life.

When it comes to fans of any sport, whether it's a pee-wee league or the professionals, it's clear what team (or athlete) a person or family supports by the colors they have on or the jersey they wear. Some people go so far as to paint their faces or other parts of their bodies for games. At that moment, they are living for what is displayed.

As a Christian, it is going to take more than just lip service. It is going to take more than selling wolf tickets. You have to demonstrate it with your life.

A lot of people like to say they are a Christian, and they have on the Jesus pieces—but for most of them, the Jesus that is hanging around their neck is not the Jesus in their heart.

I know, I know, you're saying do not judge these people, and I am not: their fruit shows for whom they are living.

Your words and living have to be the same. Attending church has to be more than just a weekend event or just something that we do; it has to be a part of our everyday life. Just like going to work and living to accomplish your dreams, the way you know who you are living for is based on the decisions you make and why you make them. Once you say yes to Christ, you start to live.

> **Romans 8:11-14** – *"And if the Spirit of him who raised Jesus from the dead is living in you, he who raised Christ from the dead will also give life to your mortal bodies because of his Spirit who lives in you. Therefore, brothers and sisters, we have an obligation – but it is not to the flesh, to live according to it. For if you live according to the flesh, you will die; but if by the Spirit you put to death the misdeeds of the body, you will live. For those who are led by the Spirit of God are children of God."* (NIV)

How do you live or surrender your will to Him every day?

Galatians 2:20 – *"I have been crucified with Christ, and I no longer live, but Christ lives in me. The life I now live in the body, I live by faith in the Son of God, who loved me and gave himself for me."* (CSB)

In closing, I want you to remember that you can survive as a Christian in today's society, but you have to give your life over to God and allow Him to lead and guide you.

NOTE PAGE

ENDORSEMENTS

"Pastor Reginald Robinson teaches us the practical application of 'S.U.R.V.I.V.A.L.' This down-to-earth book gives the reader a step-by-step walk through the Christian life."

— DAVID SEDLACEK, PhD, LMSW, CFLE;
Professor of Family Ministry and Discipleship,
Seventh-day Adventist Theological Seminary at
Andrews University.

"Pastor Reginald Robinson has written a very practical guide for survival — not so much about physical but rather, spiritual survival. The book is easy to follow and highly relevant, as it involves real-life discoveries. The author desires to help people make appropriate decisions and to walk in the right direction.

"Teaming up with Christ is crucial because survival is impossible without the trainer, safeguard, and everyday companion to whom Pastor Robinson introduces you. The information that this book brings together is a must-read for everyone who does not want his or her relationship with God to be hindered. It leads you, step-by-step, through useful

knowledge that will actually strengthen your walk with God by cultivating a strong and healthy friendship with Him.

"I strongly recommend this concrete and stress-free understanding of how to live a balanced and happy life."

— Jiří Moskala, BA, MTh, ThD, PhD, Professor of Old Testament Exegesis and Theology, Dean, Andrews University

About the Author

Reginald E. Robinson is a simple man that loves the Lord and wants to live in full service to Him by introducing Jesus to everyone he meets. He has served in several capacities in the church throughout the years. Each position has strengthened his faith and passion for winning souls for Christ. With his wife Cynthia, they founded "S.U.R.V.I.V.A.L. Ministries." They hope that with this ministry they can teach people about "surviving every day with Jesus."

Connect with the Author:

    Facebook: Survival Ministry
    Instagram: @srvalmn
    Twitter: @survalmn0410

www.ingramcontent.com/pod-product-compliance
Lightning Source LLC
Chambersburg PA
CBHW052124110526
44592CB00013B/1747